IT'S TIME TO EAT A DURIAN

It's Time to Eat a Durian

Walter the Educator

Silent King Books
A WhichHead Entertainment Imprint

Copyright © 2024 by Walter the Educator

All rights reserved. No part of this book may be reproduced in any manner whatsoever without written per- mission except in the case of brief quotations embodied in critical articles and reviews.

First Printing, 2024

Disclaimer

This book is a literary work; the story is not about specific persons, locations, situations, and/or circumstances unless mentioned in a historical context. Any resemblance to real persons, locations, situations, and/or circumstances is coincidental. This book is for entertainment and informational purposes only. The author and publisher offer this information without warranties expressed or implied. No matter the grounds, neither the author nor the publisher will be accountable for any losses, injuries, or other damages caused by the reader's use of this book. The use of this book acknowledges an understanding and acceptance of this disclaimer.

It's Time to Eat a Durian is a little collectible souvenir book that belongs to the Celebrating Cities Book Series by Walter the Educator. Collect them all and more books at WaltertheEducator.com

USE THE EXTRA SPACE TO TAKE NOTES AND DOCUMENT YOUR MEMORIES

DURIAN

It's time to eat, the sun's so bright,

It's Time to Eat a
Durian

The day is golden, full of light,

In the kitchen, waiting there,

Is a fruit beyond compare.

A spiky shell, a golden hue,

It's called Durian, it's something new,

With a smell that's strong and mighty bold,

But inside, treasures do unfold.

Come gather 'round, my little friends,

Our adventure now begins,

We'll crack it open, don't be shy,

There's more than meets the curious eye.

The shell is sharp, but don't you fear,

We'll cut it open, slice it clear,

Inside there's fruit, so soft and sweet,

A tasty, creamy, special treat.

It's Time to Eat a
Durian

It smells like dreams from distant lands,

With flavors rich like warmest sands,

Some say it's cheese, or maybe cake,

But oh, the joy it soon will make.

The taste is like a sunny day,

With whispers of a sweet bouquet,

A mix of honey, cream, and love,

As if it's sent from stars above.

Take a bite, now, don't delay,

Let the flavors dance and play,

It's creamy, smooth, with just a twist,

Of something magical, not to miss.

Some might say it's not their style,

But try it once, and wear a smile,

For durian is a fruit so rare,

It's Time to Eat a
Durian

With a taste that's beyond compare.

If you find the smell too strong,

Just close your eyes, it won't be long,

The flavor's worth the little test,

This fruit is truly one of the best.

It's time to eat, our plates are full,

This durian makes us feel so cool,

We're brave, we're strong, we tried something new,

It's Time to Eat a Durian

And now it's part of me and you.

ABOUT THE CREATOR

Walter the Educator is one of the pseudonyms for Walter Anderson. Formally educated in Chemistry, Business, and Education, he is an educator, an author, a diverse entrepreneur, and he is the son of a disabled war veteran. "Walter the Educator" shares his time between educating and creating. He holds interests and owns several creative projects that entertain, enlighten, enhance, and educate, hoping to inspire and motivate you. Follow, find new works, and stay up to date with Walter the Educator™

at WaltertheEducator.com

www.ingramcontent.com/pod-product-compliance
Lightning Source LLC
LaVergne TN
LVHW051925060526
838201LV00062B/4692